Blockchain Technology Explained

A Beginner's Guide to Blockchain Technology

ALWYN BISHOP

Copyright 2018 by Author - All rights reserved.

This document is geared towards providing exact and reliable information in regards to the topic and issue covered. The publication is sold with the idea that the publisher is not required to render accounting, officially permitted, or otherwise, qualified services. If advice is necessary, legal or professional, a practiced individual in the profession should be ordered.

- From a Declaration of Principles which was accepted and approved equally by a Committee of the American Bar Association and a Committee of Publishers and Associations.

In no way is it legal to reproduce, duplicate, or transmit any part of this document in either electronic means or in printed format. Recording of this publication is strictly prohibited and any storage of this document is not allowed unless with written permission from the publisher. All rights reserved.

The information provided herein is stated to be truthful and consistent, in that any liability, in terms of inattention or otherwise, by any usage or abuse of any policies, processes, or directions contained within is the solitary and utter responsibility of the recipient reader. Under no circumstances will any legal responsibility or blame be held against the publisher for any reparation, damages, or monetary loss due to the information herein, either directly or indirectly.

Respective authors own all copyrights not held by the publisher.

The information herein is offered for informational purposes solely, and is universal as so. The presentation of the information is without contract or any type of guarantee assurance.

The trademarks that are used are without any consent, and the publication of the trademark is without permission or backing by the trademark owner. All trademarks and brands within this book are for clarifying purposes only and are the owned by the owners themselves, not affiliated with this document.

Contents

Introduction

Chapter One – The Invention of Blockchain

Chapter Two – Usage Benefits of Blockchain for Companies and Users

Chapter Three – Terms of Blockchain Technology

Chapter Four – Companies Involved in Blockchain Technology

Chapter Five – Blockchain Technology's Future

Conclusion

Introduction

Cryptocurrency, blockchain, hashes – it might all sound like Greek to you, but by the end of this book, you should understand what all of those terms mean in depth, as well as why understanding blockchain technology is imperative for the future. You may be asking yourself what blockchain technology is, at this point.

Blockchain technology has been described as a new internet. The old internet allowed information to be shared, but that information was copied at the same time. With blockchain technology, digital information is distributed to users, but it's not copied.

Perhaps the most infamous company using blockchain technology is a cryptocurrency company by the name of Bitcoin. But now that the technical community is beginning to understand how blockchain technology works, they are devising ways to use it for many other platforms.

You don't need to know the extensive details of blockchain in order to use it, but understanding the basic workings of blockchain technology will demonstrate to you why this new internet is so revolutionary. Imagine a spreadsheet in your favorite spreadsheet program. Picture it being duplicated thousands of times across many different connected computers. Then, imagine the network of computers is designed to update this spreadsheet on a regular basis. That is the basic understanding of a blockchain. Information held on the blockchain is a shared and continually updated database.

Using the network in this manner has some obvious advantages. The database is not stored in a single position, meaning the archives that are kept are public and easily verified. A centralized version of the data doesn't exist for a hacker to corrupt. And the data is accessible to anyone on the internet because the data is held by millions of workstations at the same time. Nothing can be lost again, no one is able to control the information singularly, and there is not a single point of failure.

The old internet has been around for just about thirty years, and it has many more flaws than the new internet. Imagine an internet where none of your data is ever lost again, and your financial information stays with financial institutes, not the ill-intentioned.

The first question you might have about blockchain technology is who invented this? Unfortunately, that is an unanswered question many individuals, good and bad, are attempting to answer. While the exact 'who' behind the technology is still unknown, what it is and how it works is readily available information. Let's take a look at the invention of blockchain technology, and move on to the benefits, blockchain terminology, companies utilizing blockchain technology, and how it will affect the future in the remainder of the book.

Chapter One – The Invention of Blockchain

Satoshi Nakamoto is the most infamous pseudonym associated with blockchain technology; however, this individual – or group – is not the inventor of blockchain technology. The notion of blockchain technology is retraceable to W. Scott Stornetta and Stuart Haber in the year 1991 in their white paper *How to time-stamp a digital document.*

In this paper, they claim a digital document can be protected with a time-stamp to the data so that a user cannot back-date or forward-date the information, even if he or she is using time-stamping services. This protects the privacy of the data, as well as requires no record-keeping by the time-stamping service, making the document completely private. The incorporation of Merkle trees allowed several documents to be collected into a block; thus, the name blockchain technology.

However, while these two are the original brainstormers of this idea, the term blockchain technology did not gain significance until the year 2008, when Satoshi Nakamoto published a white paper about Bitcoin. A practical incentive was given to blockchain technology, and the issue of double spending was solved.

There are many individuals who have been suspected of being Satoshi Nakamoto, but none of them will admit to being a part of the blockchain technology revolution.

These individuals are Dorian Nakamoto, Nick Szabo, and Hal Finney.

In 2014, a reporter published a story about a computer engineer of Japanese descent living in California, Dorian Nakamoto. His real name is Satoshi Nakamoto. His link to Japan pointed toward him being the creator of blockchain technology, and the publisher of the Bitcoin white paper, because the P2P Foundation profile of the pseudonym Nakamoto identified him as a 37-year-old man living in Japan. When asked about his involvement with Bitcoin, Dorian responded that he was no longer involved with it, and it had been turned over to other people. His excuse for saying this during the interview was he thought the interviewer was asking him about his work as a military contractor.

In December of 2013, stylometric analysis was used by Skye Grey to come to the conclusion that Nick Szabo was Satoshi Nakamoto. Nick Szabo had published a paper called *Bit Gold* that was followed by the white paper on bitcoin. In the 90's, Szabo liked to use pseudonyms when publishing papers about decentralized currency.

Lastly, Hal Finney was a cryptographic pioneer before bitcoin was established. He was the first person to use bitcoin, make improvements to the code, and file bug reports. He was Dorian Nakamoto's neighbor. Writing analysis compared samples of Nakamoto's writing to Finney's writing, and came to the conclusion they had the closest resemblance out of everyone suspected. It was concluded Finney might have been a ghostwriter on behalf of Nakamoto, or he may have used Dorian's identity.

No matter which story is true, or if all three accounts are true, blockchain technology has been unleashed on the world, and it's here to stay. So what is it?

What Is Blockchain Technology?

When it comes down to it, blockchain technology might not appear to be that different from some of the things you may already be familiar with on the web, such as Wikipedia. Using blockchain technology, many people can write an entry into a record of data, and a group of users is able to control how that record of data is changed and updated. Similarly, Wikipedia articles are not the creation of one publisher. A single person does not have a monopoly over the information.

However, upon further inspection, the differences that make the blockchain technology so different are more prevalent. While both run on a distributed network — the internet — Wikipedia has been built on the World Wide Web using a client-server network model. A client — user — with permission associated with an account can change Wikipedia entries stored on a centralized server.

Whenever someone accesses that Wikipedia page, they get the updated version of a master copy of the article. Control of that database is with the Wikipedia administrators, which allows access and permissions to be maintained by a central authority.

The digital making of Wikipedia is similar to the centralized and protected databases that banks, insurance companies, and governments retain. A single focal point of control exists with a centralized database, including access, management of updates, and protection from hackers. The distributed database by blockchain technology has a fundamental difference. This is the most important feature of blockchain technology.

The master copy of a Wikipedia article is edited on a server, and all the users are able to see that new version. With blockchain technology, every node in the network comes to the same conclusion, each recording and updating independently, with the most popular record being the official record in lieu of a master copy. There is not a centralized control center, and one single person or entity is not able to change valuable information.

This difference in blockchain technology is what makes it so unique and useful. It eliminates the need for a trusted party to aid in a digital relationship.

Despite a newfound interest in blockchain technology, it is not new.

Blockchain technology is a combination of technologies that are already proven to work, but it's applied in a new manner. It's the orchestration of three technologies – the internet, private key cryptography, protocol governing incentivization – that have made blockchain technology so useful.

The result is a system of digital interactions that don't need a trusted third party. The work of securing a digital relationship is implicit.

Digital Trust

Trust is a risk judgment between two parties, and in the digital world, determining trust pertains to identity and proving permissions, authentication, and authorization respectively. To put it in simpler terms, one party wants to know if the other party is who they say they are and if that party is allowed to do what they are trying to do.

In blockchain technology's case, private key cryptography offers a powerful ownership tool that fulfills the authentication requirements. Possession of the private key is ownership. In addition, it spares the parties from having to share more personal information than they would need for an exchange, which might leave them exposed to a hacker.

However, authentication is not enough. Authorization, such as broadcasting the right transaction type, or having the funds in the bank, needs a peer-to-peer, distributed network as a beginning point. A distributed network lessens the risk of centralized failure or corruption.

This distributed network has to be committed to the transaction network's security and recordkeeping. Authorizing a transaction is a result of the entire network applying the rules it was designed on – the blockchain's protocol.

Authentication and authorization used in this manner let interactions happen in the digital world without relying on trust. Today, industries and entrepreneurs across the globe have realized the implications of blockchain technology and what it offers – powerful and previously unheard of digital relationships can exist. Blockchain technology is described as the backbone for a transaction layer for the internet and the foundation of the internet of value.

How Does Blockchain Technology Work?

You understand what blockchain technology is and what it offers now, but how does it work exactly?

There are three components that make up a blockchain. None of these components are new, but it's their application and orchestration that's new. These technologies are private key cryptography, an incentive to service the network's transactions, security, and record-keeping, and a distributed network with a shared ledger.

Cryptographic Keys

Let's say two people want to enter a transaction through the internet. Each of them has a private key and a public key. The main purpose of blockchain technology's cryptographic keys is to make a secure digital identity reference. The identity of the individuals in the transaction is based on the possession of a combination of both private and public cryptographic keys.

The combination of these keys can be seen as a form of consent, which creates a useful digital signature. In turn, this signature provides control of ownership. However, strong control of ownership isn't enough to secure a digital relationship. While the authentication problem has been solved, it has to be combined with a means of approving a transaction and permission.

For blockchain technology, this starts with a distributed network.

Distributed Network

The advantage and need for a distributed network are understandable if you use the 'if a tree falls in the forest' thought experiment. This experiment asks that if a tree falls in the forest, with cameras to record that fall, then we can be certain the tree fell. There is visual evidence the tree has fallen, even if the why or the how might not be certain.

The value of bitcoin blockchain technology is that it's a large network where validators, such as the camera in the tree falling analogy, reach an agreement they've witnessed the same thing at the same time. Rather than cameras, they're using mathematical verification in blockchain technology. The size of the network is imperative in securing the network.

That's one of blockchain technology's most attractive qualities. It's so large and has obtained so much computing power.

When a cryptographic key is combined with this network, a useful form of digital interactions comes about. The process starts with taking the private key, making an announcement, and attaching it to the other user's public key.

A block with a digital signature, timestamp, and relevant information is broadcast to the nodes in the network.

Incentive

Realists tend to challenge the tree falling in the woods thought experiment with a question. Why would there be a million computers with cameras waiting to record whether that tree has fallen? How would computing power to service the network to make it secure be attracted?

For an open, public blockchain, this involves mining, such as with bitcoin. Mining is created off the exclusive approach to the age-old question of economics.

With a blockchain, by a user offering his or her computer processing power to service the network, there is a reward available for the computer. A person's selfishness is being used in order to help the public need for the processing of the blockchain.

As with Bitcoin, the objective of the procedure is to get rid of the risk that the same bitcoin is spent in a separate transaction at the same time, in such a way that this might be hard to spot.

This is the way bitcoin is supposed to act as property or gold. Bitcoins and their base units have to be distinctive to be owned and have a worth. To do this, the nodes serving the network make and preserve an account of transactions for every bitcoin by working to solve mathematical equations that represent proof-of-work.

Basically, the nodes are voting with their computer power, expressing an agreement about new blocks or rejecting an invalid block. When a majority of the miners come to the same conclusion, they add a new block to the chain. The block is timestamped, and it can contain messages or data.

The amount, type, and verification can be different for every blockchain. TI's a matter of protocol, or rules for what is and isn't a valid transaction or a valid creation of a new block. The verification process is tailored for every blockchain. Any necessary rules and incentives can be made when enough nodes arrive at the same conclusion no how transactions should be verified.

Armed with the basic information of what blockchain technology is and how it works, let's move forward to how blockchain technology can benefits users and companies.

Chapter Two – Usage Benefits of Blockchain for Companies and Users

Did you know bitcoins traded for $1 back in 2011, and recently, they traded for $16,000 for a single bitcoin? You may or may not be interested in purchasing and trading bitcoin as a form of investment, but the fundamental technology that makes bitcoin conceivable – the blockchain – is something everyone should appreciate.

The blockchain is a public, virtual archive that chronicles information in a protected and apparent manner. Dissimilar to banks that enable a transaction with a traditional currency, the blockchain lets the transfer of cryptocurrency happen in a free and decentralized setting. All that data is held in an interlinked network of computers, owned and run by the users involved in the data.

Benefits of Blockchain Technology to Industries

Some entrepreneurs see blockchain technology as more promising than the cryptocurrency it was designed for. Yes, the demand for bitcoin is huge right now, but because it's supported by nothing but sentiment, at this point, it's sensible to think the bitcoin bubble could pop like the real estate bubble. The advantages of blockchain technology, however, are more than good enough to support this technology's significance for many generations. Let's take a look at how blockchain technology can be beneficial to many different industries.

1. **Supply chain management**

Blockchain technology offers a great amount of benefits for supply chain management, such as traceability and cost-effectiveness. Blockchains can be used to track the original of goods, movement, quantity, and so much more. This brings about transparency in the business-to-business economy by simplifying processes such as production process assurance, ownership transfer, and payments.

2. **Quality assurance**

If a user detects an irregularity somewhere in the supply chain, then a blockchain system will lead that user to the point of origin of that irregularity. This makes it easier for a business to carry out an investigation and perform the necessary corrections.

3. **Accounting**

Recording a transaction through a blockchain will eliminate human error and protect financial data from tampering. Keep in mind the records are verified each time they're passed from one blockchain node to the next node. This process will leave a highly traceable audit trail, too.

The entire account process will become more efficient on a foundational level. Instead of keeping separate records, business will keep a single, joint record. The integrity of the company's financial information will be guaranteed.

4. Smart contracts

Contractual transactions can slow down the processes of some businesses, especially those that process a lot of communication on a consistent basis. With a smart contract, an agreement can be validated quickly, signed, and enforced with a blockchain. This eliminates the need for a mediator, which saves the company money and time.

In the present, blockchain solutions, such as credits, offer smart contracts coupled with an in-house cryptocurrency. By merging it all into a single platform, a business can combine services without revealing a large amount of proprietary information to a third party.

5. Voting

Just as with supply chain management, blockchains benefit the voting process because they can be trusted. Right now, opportunities pertaining to government elections are being looked into. One example of this is Moscow's government, who is testing blockchains at the local election level. Doing this diminishes the likelihood of electoral fraud significantly, which is still a major issue despite the numerous electronic voting systems in place.

Another example would be when NASDAQ used blockchain technology for shareholder voting. It worked when they provided local governments with identity cards.

6. Stock exchange

The idea of using blockchains for commodities and securities trading has been around for some time. Given the open, yet reliable, nature of these systems, it's not surprising to hear that stock exchanges are now considering it as the next step.

Australia's stock exchange is already set on switching their system over to a blockchain system, which has been designed by Digital Asset Holdings. In December 2017, a press release published by Blythe Master, CEO of Digital Asset, said that after so much hype surrounding the distributed ledger technology, their announcement delivered the first solid proof that blockchain technology was able to live up to its potential.

7. Energy supply

Two types of businesses exist on this planet – the ones who don't care about their monthly utility bills and the ones who wonder where their huge energy expenditures are coming from.

In certain parts of the world, households and commercial businesses can take advantage of a blockchain-enabled transactive grid for sustainable energy solutions that track usage accurately. A few examples might be Powerpeers in the Exergy and Netherlands in Brooklyn. Blockchain can be used to advance tracking clean energy. Once the electricity is directed to the grid, no one is able to distinguish if it's generated by fossil fuels, wind, or solar energy.

In a traditional sense, renewable energy is traced through tradable certificates issued by governments. These certificates are not very good at serving their purpose, but it's something blockchain can handle easily.

8. Peer-to-peer global transactions

Lastly, the great rise of Bitcoin and other cryptocurrency markets out there are not without merit. The main benefit is the ability to quickly, securely, and cheaply transfer money across the globe.

While many other services, such as PayPal, allow for international payments to be processed, these companies require a sizeable fee for every transaction. Other peer-to-peer payment services have limitations, such as minimum amounts and location restrictions. That's why many organizations, as well as consumers, are starting to prefer cryptocurrency for an international transfer. Not only are they more secure, but users are given more freedom when it comes to the movement of their money.

Benefits of Decentralized Blockchain Technology

It's obvious that blockchain technology is making strides in many other industries outside of cryptocurrency. But let's take a look at how decentralized blockchain technology benefits the average user.

1. **Prevention of fraud**

Due to blockchains being open-sourced ledgers, and due to every transaction being recorded on them, it's easy to tell if fraud is happening. The integrity of a blockchain system is maintained and monitored by miners who are validating the transactions day in and day out. There are thousands of miners who are validating transactions on the blockchain all around the world at any given moment. This gives the decentralized blockchain cryptocurrencies a large amount of oversight and makes them immune to fraud. This is a huge benefit of decentralized blockchain technology.

2. **Protection from government interference**

Cryptocurrencies based on blockchain technology are not controlled by a government entity, bank, or a central bank. This means they are not able to be interfered with by a government. Government interference is a problem that's led to the devaluations of numerous currencies in history, such as the Denarius in the Roman Empire, or the German Mark in Weimar Germany, or the Zimbabwean Dollar in recent history. Bad things happen to currencies when governments interfere with them too much.

One issue that often happens when governments meddle with currencies is they end up becoming inflated by devaluing, debasing, or printing too much currency in a short amount of time. With a decentralized blockchain, it's not possible for a government to interfere with a cryptocurrency because they do not have control over the technology. No one has control. This is due to cryptocurrencies being software programs with a finite amount of currency. This makes it difficult for hyperinflation to occur, unlike national fiat currency.

3. Faster transaction times

A blockchain-based cryptocurrency will provide transaction times that are much quicker than a bank transaction time. For example, wire transfers can take days for the transaction to go through. However, a transaction made using blockchain technology takes just a few minutes. The fact that a transaction is faster through a blockchain-based cryptocurrency without losing accuracy is beneficial for many individuals and businesses across the globe.

If money is able to flow quicker, then moves are made much quicker, decisions are made faster, and goods can go from one point to the next much faster. Increased transaction speed is a good thing for our global economy.

4. Increased financial proficiency

A decentralized blockchain allows a transaction to be made directly from one person to the other, without a third-party interfering. This improves financial proficiency and lets individuals be less reliant on a bank or another financial institution. This saves people a lot of money in fees and other costs associated with using a bank.

5. Effective way to store value

Bitcoin has been referred to as digital gold. That's because many of its features are of that of gold. For example, there is a finite amount of it, it needs to be mined, it's desirable in numerous countries, and so on and so forth. Due to its qualities and the fact that it's digital gold, bitcoin and blockchain technology can be an effective way to store value. Many individuals have realized this, and that's why the value of bitcoin has soared in recent years.

In addition, blockchain-based currencies have a single advantage over gold and other precious metals as a store of value. Bitcoin and other cryptocurrencies can be stored on a mobile device or computer and sent over the internet. This means people do not have to purchase security deposit boxes or safes at a bank to store their wealth.

If utilized correctly, blockchain technology is an excellent solution to many of today's current complications in business, banking, and government operations. You understand what blockchain technology is and how it can benefit you, so what do all those weird terms mean? Let's take a look at that in the following chapter.

Chapter Three – Terms of Blockchain Technology

Many of the terms found in blockchain articles and books are programming or technical terms, actually. If you're familiar with computer science, then some of these terms may be a little repetitive, but many who are curious about blockchain technology are not as technologically savvy as a computer programmer. However, understanding what different terms mean can help any individual navigate the world of blockchains and cryptocurrency efficiently.

For example, blockchain and bitcoin are used interchangeably, but in reality, the bitcoin system utilizes blockchain technology. And while bitcoin utilizes blockchain technology, that doesn't mean every program that uses blockchains is a cryptocurrency like bitcoin. Blockchains can be used for many different forms of recording information. Let's look at some of the terms you're most likely to come across in the world of blockchain technology.

Address

In Bitcoin, addresses are long strings of alphanumeric characters used to send, receive, and hold money. To confirm the contract, a bitcoin wallet owner has two encrypted keys, a private key and public key. For bitcoin wallets, the wallet address is public and the privet key is necessary to verify with the entire system that a digital signature is confirmed and the transaction is a legal one.

Altcoins

This is an abbreviation of the Bitcoin alternative. Right now, the majority of altcoins are forks with minor changes to the POW algorithm of the blockchain. The most well-known altcoin is Litecoin. Litecoin introduced changes tot eh original Bitcoin protocol like increased maximum number of coins, a decreased block generation time, and a different hashing algorithm.

ASIC

ASIC stands for application specific integrated circuit, and it's a silicon chip that's designed to do just one task. In the case of Bitcoin, ASICs are intended to solve SHA-256 hashing questions in order to mine a new bitcoin. ASICs are considered more efficient than the usual hardware, such as CPUs and GPUs. Using a regular computer to mine Bitcoin is not profitable and only results in a higher utility bill.

Bitcoin

Bitcoin is not supervised by an authority or an institution and is considered a decentralized currency. It's not controlled by a single entity, which is why it's aid that those who participate in the system are the ones who control it. Yet, at the same time, no one controls it. Bitcoin is an open code that is identified through anonymous and ciphered codes rather than coins and bills. It lets all types of financial transactions be registered in a secure environment amongst equals due to it using peer-to-peer technology.

Blockchain technology was first made as a core element of bitcoin, which made it the first digital currency to solve the double spending issue without the need of a central server or trusted authority. The value of bitcoin is phenomenal.

There is a growing number of suppliers who are accepting bitcoin as a form of payment. All types of products and services are able to be purchased with this cryptocurrency. For examples, Microsoft lets customers use bitcoin to purchase games, applications, and videos on Windows phones, gaming systems, and computers. Overstock allows customers to purchase furniture, jewelry, and appliances. Due to the steady increase in the price over the last few months, bitcoin's use as a means of payment is decreasing.

The word Bitcoin is used to refer to the protocol that utilizes blockchain and to the peer-to-peer network that supports it.

Block

A transaction on a blockchain is combined into a single block, and every ten minutes, a new block of around 1MB is made. Every block in the blockchain has four parts – a timestamp, reference to the previous block, a summary of the transaction, and the Proof of Work that went into make the secure block.

Secure hashing means that editing a block without making a change in the subsequent block isn't possible. No person or company is able to go into the bitcoin network and complete a successful allocation worth millions of dollars due to two reasons. First, the block requires independent confirmations. Second, answering the mathematical calculations for the cryptographic problems is hard, necessitating special miners.

Block Explorer

This is an online tool used to explore the blockchain of a specific cryptocurrency. It allows you to watch and follow the live transactions that are occurring on the blockchain. A block explorer can serve as a blockchain analysis and provide information like total network hash rate, transaction growth, coin supply, and more.

Block Reward

Block rewards are an amount of cryptocurrency a miner obtains for processing a transaction in a block. Due to the mining of blocks being so crucial to the security of the Bitcoin network, the Bitcoin protocol has a mechanism to encourage users to mine. Each time a block is added, the miner who found that block is given 12.5 BTC as a block reward. This number will change as time goes on.

Chain Linking

Chain linking is connecting two blockchains to one another, which allows transactions between the chains to occur. This lets blockchains, such as Bitcoin, communicate with other sidechains, which allows the exchange of assets between the chains.

Client

A client is a software program a user executes on a computer, laptop, or a mobile device in order to launch an application.

Cloud Mining

Classic cryptocurrency mining requires an individual to invest a large amount of electricity and hardware into the system. Cloud mining companies hope to make mining accessible to everyone. A user can log into a website and invest money in the company that already has mining datacenters. The money's managed by the company and invested in the mining equipment. Investors get a share of the revenue. The disadvantage of cloud mining is that users obtain a low return compared to traditional mining.

Consortium Blockchains

These are blockchains where the consent process is determined by a preselected set of nodes. For example, a consortium of fifteen financial organizations, each one with a node, might require ten nodes to sign every block for the block to be binding. The right to read the blockchain might be public or restricted to participants. There're hybrid routes like the root hashes of the blocks being public together with an API that lets public members make a limited number of queries and get back cryptographic proofs of some segments of the blockchain state. These blockchains could be considered partially decentralized.

Cryptocurrency

Cryptocurrency is similar to money or cash in that it's a means of exchange. The only difference is cryptocurrency is digital. The first cryptocurrency started in 2009 – Bitcoin – by Satoshi Nakamoto, who created the basis of the system. From that moment on, other cryptocurrencies began popping up with different characteristics and specifications, which will be discussed later on in this book. There is more than 1,000 cryptocurrencies on the market, but we're going to look at the more popular ones only.

Cryptojacking

This is a stealthy use of a computer to mine cryptocurrency. The first broadly recognized effort to do this was on Piratebay. They allowed an in-browser mining software so that when someone visited the website, their computer started mining cryptocurrency using the browser. The users would begin noticing unusual behavior on their computer, and Piratebay removed the program.

There have been some attempts to do this since Piratebay. The easiest way to discover if a device is mining cryptocurrency is to inspect the task manager for any unusual CPU performance or using the debug console of the browser to look for a mining script. Creators released Chrome browser applications to guard users from mining using their devices.

Decentralized Application (dApp)

In order for an application to be considered decentralized, it has to meet the following criteria.

1. The application has to be entirely open-source, function alone, and have no entity governing the bulk of the tokens. The program can adjust the protocol in reaction to suggested enhancements and market response, but all the changes have to be decided by an agreement of its users.
2. The application information and records of operation have to be cryptographically stored in a decentralized, public blockchain in order to avoid a central point of failure.
3. The application has to use a cryptographic token that is essential for admission to the application, and any input of value from miners has to be satisfied with the application's tokens.
4. The application has to produce tokens conferring to a standard algorithm that acts as proof of value, such as Bitcoin's Proof of Work Algorithm.

Decentralized Autonomous Organization (DAOs)

A decentralized autonomous organization is a fully automated business entity, which is a decentralized network of narrow-AI autonomous agents that perform production function that maximizes output and divides its work into computationally inflexible responsibilities that incentivize humans to do and tasks that it performs itself.

These forms of organizations can be thought of as corporations that are run without human involvement and are under the control of an incorruptible set of business rules. These rules are applied as publicly auditable open-source software managed across the computers of their investors. People become the stakeholders by purchasing stock in the organization or being paid in the stock of the organization to provide services for that organization. The stock can entitle the owners to a share of the profits of the decentralized autonomous organization, participate in its growth, or have a say in how it's run.

Digital Signature

Digital signatures are used for signing a transaction. Every time a transaction is sent to the blockchain, it is signed by the user's private key. This signed transaction is when sent over the network with a corresponding public key. Every miner can verify the signature by verifying it with the public key.

Double Spending

Double spending happens when an individual successfully spends money more than once. Bitcoin was the first to implement a solution to this in 2009. The solution verifies every transaction added to the blockchain in order to prevent double spending.

Ethereum

Ethereum is another decentralized platform that allows the creation of smart contracts. Some call Ethereum a decentralized supercomputer. Ethereum runs on its own blockchain and was originally created as an improved version that would surpass the programming limits of Bitcoin.

Ethereum codifies data the same way as Bitcoin, but one of the important differences is that it's able to be used to create smart contracts, which are pieces of software that automate and shield the execution of previously created orders. In addition, Ethereum has a vast variety of applications beyond those related to finance. The cryptocurrency of Ethereum is Ether, the second most popular after Bitcoin.

Encryption

In the computer world, encryption is the action of securing data in such a way that's it's only interpretable by a device with a password or code. Ciphering is the same thing in cryptography. It's a technique that lets a user protect the exchange of information or data in which the processes where they are used are more secure.

Forks

The strength of a public blockchain network relies on the democratic nature of the blockchain. Everything is decentralized, and all parties have the exact same information. No single person is above another. However, that asset has a roundabout weakness. If every bit of information in the blockchain is decentralized, and everyone has to approve of the changes, then you cannot change anything or improve anything. If you centralized in order to make changes, then the nature of blockchain is being attacked.

This paradox has created a consequence, known as forks. When one part of the network users desires to make a change, and they come across the opposition of others, the resulting impossibility of finding unanimous positions creates forks in the blockchain networks.

Bitcoin experienced a fork on August 1, 2017, after an argument about the size of the blocks in the blockchain, which created the Bitcoin Cash (BCC). Another fork is the one that happened in Ethereum in 2016; at the time, a hacker attack was found in a programming mistake that created a divide of the network into Ethereum classic and Ethereum. Lately, the code has been updated with a fork. This time, it was a planned one created to make a general improvement to the platform. This was the first stage of a greater update that would include changes to increase the efficiency.

Genesis Block

A genesis block is the first block in the blockchain.

Halving

Halving is the decrease in the block payment that is given to the cryptocurrency miners after a certain amount of blocks are mined. Bitcoin's block mining return splits every 210,000 blocks.

Hash

Miners must validate groups of blocks in the blockchain. To do this, a miner has to find a digital fingerprint or a password that identifies them. This digital fingerprint is known as a hash. It is unique, unmodifiable, and not repeatable. Every time a new hash is discovered, it's distributed to the rest of the nodes in the network, so they're always in sync.

ICOs

Initial Coin Offerings, or ICOs, are a type of company financing. The oddness is that companies offer tokens rather than shares, and shareholders pay with digital coins using a blockchain. However, due to the lack of regulation of this type of financing, at times, these tokens do not represent the shares or real economic rights of a company that issues the ICO.

InterPlanetary File System (IPFS)

IPFSs are a hypermedia distribution protocol that is addressed by content and identities. An IPFS allows the creation of completely distributed applications. It strives to make the web quicker, more secure, and more open. IPFS is an open-source project that was created by the team at InterPlanetary Networks in cooperation with many contributors from the open-source community.

This program is a P2P dispersed file system that connects computers with the same system of records. In some ways, it's similar to the internet, but IPFS can be viewed as a solitary BitTorrent swarm, swapping data in the Git repository. In layman's terms, IPFS offers a high amount of data content-addressed block storage model that has content-addressed links. This creates a general Merkle DAG, a data assembly where you can build versioned file systems and blockchains.

Lightning Network

The Lightning Network is a decentralized network that uses smart contracts on the blockchain network in order to allow instant payments across a network of users. The Lightning Network allows bitcoin transactions to occur instantly without having to worry about block confirmation times. It lets millions of transactions happen in just a few seconds, at a low cost, and between different blockchains, as long as both chains are using the same hash function. The Lightning network allows two users on the network to make a ledger entry, conduct a number of transactions between themselves, and after the process is done, they can record the state of the transactions on the blockchain. For now, the bitcoin network can handle up to seven transactions every second. As a comparison, the

Visa payment network can complete 45,000 transactions every second during a holiday period. This protocol attempts to solve the bitcoin scalability issue.

Merkle Tree

Merkle trees have the basic idea of having a piece of information that is linked to another. This can be done by linking things together with a cryptographic hash. The content can be used to determine the hash. By using the hashing, the content can be addressed, and content becomes indisputable because if anything is changed in the information, then the cryptographic hash will change, and the connection is going to be altered. Bitcoin utilizes cryptographic hashing. Every block points to the preceding block, and if you change the block, then the hash changes and will make that block invalid.

Miners and Digital Mining

Mining is the process of launching new bitcoins into the market through the creation of chained blocks according to the timing set in the protocol. Those who are in charge of mining for bitcoin are referred to as miners. They use powerful computers connected twenty-four hours a day to make sure that all the transactions are performed properly. To validate the transaction and make the block, a miner has to find a hash – digital key – for every block so as to link to the next one. Every time a miner finds a cryptographic key, a bitcoin is mined, and the miner receives payment in bitcoin.

Mining Pool

In mining pools, different users will organize together to provide computing power for the bitcoin network. If a Bitcoin is created, then each one of the users in that mining pool will receive their fair share proportionally to their mining capabilities. The advantage of a mining pool is that the block rewards will be distributed across the pool, which provides a more stable income.

Node

A node is a computer that forms part of the blockchain network. They're responsible for storing and distributing the updated copies of transactions. Every time a new block is created and added to the general ledger, a copy is added to the node in the network. Every miner is a node, but not all nodes are a miner.

Oracles

Smart contracts on blockchain networks can't access the outside network by themselves. Therefore, an oracle is between a smart contract and the outside world, providing the information necessary by the smart contract to prove performance while sending commands to the outside systems.

Private Blockchains

A private blockchain is one where the write permissions are kept central to a single institute. Read permissions can be restricted or public to an extent. Some applications that might be used for are auditing and database management internal to one company, so public readability becomes not necessary in these cases, but in other cases, public audibility might be necessary.

Private Key

Every time a client opens a cryptocurrency wallet, a public and private key pair will be created. The private key is an indiscriminately created number that lets a user make transactions over the blockchain. It's stored locally and kept a secret. Some people choose to print their key and keep it in a lockbox, erasing all existence from their computers.

Every time a bitcoin is sent, a private key is needed to mark the operation. This action is automatically done by the wallet software the user has chosen. When a wallet asks a user to do a backup, this means that the user has to secure their private key.

There are a few different wallets, like mobile wallets, online wallets, desktop wallets, paper wallets, and hardware wallets. The category of the wallet is determined by where the private key is stored. An online wallet is provided by exchanges and keeps the user's private keys on their servers. If the service provider is offline, a user will lose access to their funds. A hardware wallet stores a user's private key in a secure device that looks like a USB flash drive.

Proof of Authority

This is a consent tool in a private blockchain that gives a client or a number of clients with a specific private key the right to make all the blocks in the blockchain.

Proof of Work

Proof of Work or POW is a requirement that expensive computations have to be made in order to support a transaction. POW exists to allow trustless agreement. A hashed block is a POW.

Ring Signature

The ring signature is a cryptographic technology that can provide a level of anonymity on a blockchain. Ring signatures ensure a transaction output on the blockchain is not able to be traced. Messages signed with ring signatures are endorsed by someone in a particular set of people. One of the security properties of ring signatures is that they should be computationally infeasible to figure out which one of the group members' keys were used to create the signature.

Sidechains

These are blockchains that are interoperable with one another and with Bitcoin. This helps avoid liquidity shortages, fragmentation, security breaches, market fluctuations, and outright fraud associated with an alternative cryptocurrency. A sidechain is a new blockchain that is backed by Bitcoin using Bitcoin contracts, just like dollars, yen, and pounds are backed by gold. Thousands of sidechains could be backed by Bitcoin, all with different purposes and characteristics, and all of them taking advantage of the scarcity and resilience guaranteed by the Bitcoin blockchain.

Smart Contract

Smart contracts are digital agreements stored on the blockchain that are not able to be altered once they are signed. It defines a logical operation that has to be fulfilled in order to perform a task, such as a deposit of money or information.

Let's look at an example, conditions of releasing money to a third party delivery team. Perhaps a sender wishes to send information to a receiver using a third party, but they want to pay money for the delivery only after the delivery has occurred. Then, a smart contract might operate as follows. The source pays the shipment cash on the day of the creation of information. The smart contract holds compensation to the delivery crew until the recipient tells the sender they have received the information. Only then will a smart contract issue the payment and automatically handover that money to the delivery team.

Token

Originally, the term 'token' was the term given to chips acquired with money that was used to purchase a service or good. As an example, they might be used to purchase food at a fair or at a casino to gamble. In the blockchain world, token means the same thing, but it's in the virtual sense. A token is a unit of value that is obtained through the blockchain, and they are used to acquire goods and services.

Just like Bitcoin, tokens are transferred through a message on the blockchain network, but they can be exchanged for numerous different services. They can be used to guarantee the obtainment of future services a company promises to offer when used as initial coin offerings (ICOs) as a way to finance a startup.

Tokens are nothing more than a new term used to reference a unit of value given by a private entity. While they have many similarities with bitcoins (a value attached to them that's accepted by a community, and they're blockchain-based), they have a much greater purpose. A token is more than a currency since it can be used in many different applications. Almost all tokens depend on Ethereum's blockchain rules, which is more complete than bitcoin's blockchain protocol.

Armed with an understanding of blockchain terminology, let's go ahead and take a look at companies currently involved in blockchain technology, as well as companies who use it.

Chapter Four – Companies Involved in Blockchain Technology

Companies who use blockchain technology as a core component of their daily operations are cropping up everywhere. However, there are plenty of companies who do not utilize blockchain technology directly, but instead, use the services of the aforementioned companies. Let's look at some companies who use blockchain technology as their core business platform and those who utilize the services of those companies. Knowing the names of the players of the game gives you an edge when making investment decisions.

Companies Involved in Blockchain Technology

Since the inception of blockchain technology and Bitcoin, there have been many companies popping up across the globe that use this technology to their advantage. Understanding who they are will help you have a better knowledge-base to work with when you're exploring the world of blockchains. If you decide to invest in blockchain technology, then some of the information in this section may help you come to a more informed decision.

Ethereum

We learned what Ethereum is in the previous chapter – a decentralized platform using smart contracts, which allows users to make agreements that are executed automatically without human interference. Ethereum was launched on

July 30, 2015, by Vitalik Buterin — the winner of the 2014 World Technology Award — and Jeffrey Wilcke — the former VP of Amazon.

In 2017, every three out of four projects were on Ethereum's platform, making it the most popular platform for ICOs. About thirteen million people use Ethereum's services. The token, ETH, is the third-ranking cryptocurrency after Bitcoin and Ripple.

IOTA

IOTA is an open-source distributed ledger that specializes in the Internet of Things. The system does not have a transaction fee, has a low confirmation time, and is stable despite the number of transactions conducted on it because its technology is based on the consensus model Tangle. Tangle doesn't have blocks, chains, or minders. If you need to make a transaction, you need to approve two previous transactions appointed by the system. These actions prove the nodes have the same current state.

The project was revealed in July 2016 by David Sonstebo and Dominik Schiener. In November of 2017, IOTA joined with PwC, Deutsche Telekom, Microsoft, and others for a data monetization program. As of November 2017, IOTA's platform had over 65,000 users.

Coinbase

One of the top digital currency wallets and platforms for exchange, Coinbase's announcement that it would support

Bitcoin Cash significantly affected the Bitcoin Cash price. The platform is one out of three blockchain projects that obtained BitLicense, which is the license issued by the New York State Department of Financial Services. In 2016, it was turned into GDAX – Global Digital Asset Exchange.

The exchange is the first licensed exchanged in the United States that demonstrates its activities are dependable due to the close observation of the Securities and Exchange Commission.

The company was launched in July 2011 by Brian Armstrong and Fred Ehrsam. Brian Armstrong worked for Deloitte, Airbnb, and IBM previously, and Fred Ehrsam is a former trader at Goldman Sachs.

The exchange has over 13,300,000 users.

Ripple

Ripple's a real-time, gross settlement and currency exchange. The main goal of this program is to make an entire system that's devoted to transferring money. Created in 2012, the company is aiming to ensure real-time transactions amongst banks.

The company is working with over seventy-five banks across the globe as of now. These banks are using and testing the technology in their internal payment systems. As of December 2017, Ripple announced Japanese and South Korean banks had begun testing blockchain to make international payments between banks less costly.

The company was launched in October 2012 by Brad Garlinghouse and Stefan Thomas.

Brave

In just 27 seconds, Brave, one of the fastest ICOs, raised $35 million. This new web browser blocks trackers and advertisements. As a result, the websites work quicker, and traffic decreases greatly. Users save time and money, and they can't catch malware from an ad by clicking on it accidentally. Brendan Eich and Brian R. Bondy are the two who launched Brave in May of 2017.

Brave has around two to three million users.

Qtum

The first UTXO-based smart contract organization with a proof-of-stake consensus model, Qtum's platform uses Account Attraction Layer to merge Bitcoin's Core and Ethereum's Virtual Machine. The proof-of-stake model lowers the computational effort in the network and increases the scaling capabilities.

Qtum was launched in March 2017 by Patrick Dai, Jordan Earls, and Neil Mahi.

OmiseGO

OmiseGO was launched in June 2017 by Donnie Harinsut and Jun Hasewaga. It's a decentralized financial technology that handles exchanges and payment services. The creators developed a way to retain high token liquidity. The platform is based off Ethereum, and it's a link between gateways, payment systems, and financial organizations. While the team might not be familiar with the blockchain community, their advisers are.

Steem

This platform is a decentralized social publishing network. The user's reward depends on the number of likes a post gets. The way the community responds to a post demonstrates how an individual can improve his or her skills. Tokens can be created in the network to raise funds from the community. Dan Larimer and Ned Scott launched Steem in July 2016, and about half a million individuals are using the platform.

Augur

A prediction market platform for real events, Augur allows users to purchase shares for events that a user is sure will happen. The system is based on Ethereum, so smart contracts make sure the payments are processed. As all predictions work on public blockchain technology, no one is able to change a prediction afterward. This platform was begun in August 2015 by Joey Krug and Jack Peterson.

Golem

Golem is an open-sourced, decentralized supercomputer that is powered by the users' computers. Many industries require a lot of computations, such as DNA analysis, biology, discrete logarithm, cryptography, big data, machine learning, and much more. The service provides the power for these industries and their computations.

Golem was launched in November 2016 by Julian Zawistowski and Piotr Janiuk, and the system has reached four million users.

Companies Using Blockchain Technology

Blockchain technology is quickly being utilized for enterprise use. Because it creates and keeps a permanent transcript of an item's transactions, blockchain technology is useful for tracking company's supply chains. Using this technology rather than past methods can be more accurate and efficient, which saves business money and time. Let's look at some of the more well-known companies dabbling in blockchain technology.

Walmart

Walmart is a highly known company across the globe, and they are using blockchain to allow employees to track products back to where they originated from. After scanning a product in the store's app, an employee can see what farm a specific piece of fruit came from, as well as where that fruit is stored in their storage facilities. The technology can help customers understand where their food is coming from and might streamline the restocking process.

Maersk

Maersk is a slightly less known company to many individuals, but it's the world's largest shipping company. It completed its first test with blockchain technology in March of 2017 by looking at how blockchain technology could help manage its cargo. In the test, US Homeland Security, Dutch customs, and Maersk were able to remotely access data about the cargo, which suggests the technology could help streamline and secure international shipping.

British Airways

One of the largest airlines in the world, British Airways tested blockchain technology by seeing how it could manage data about flights between Geneva, London, and Miami in 2017. Using a single unchangeable history source, the airline aimed to reduce conflicting flight information coming from gate monitors, the airline's website, and flight apps.

UPS

UPS has just joined the Blockchain in Trucking Alliance (BiTA) in November of 2017 in the hopes of pushing for increased transparency amongst every group involved in the supply chain. The group's working to create blockchain standards for the freight industry.

FedEx

FedEx, one of the other shipping giants of the world, joined BiTA in February of 2018 and is already launching a blockchain-powdered pilot program to solve customer disputes. FedEx hopes the program will clarify what information should be stored on blockchain to best help customers with their problems. FedEx also wishes to use the technology to store records.

As you can see, blockchain technology has a lot more uses than just for cryptocurrencies. It can help store information, and it can help make sure that information is maintained and kept accurate. Data cannot be corrupted because a single individual hacks into the system, and many companies across the globe are starting to see how that can benefit their bottom line, as well as their customers and clients.

Backing by these large companies is helping facilitate the future of blockchain technology.

Chapter Five – Blockchain Technology's Future

Knowing the future is impossible, but there are many educated guesses as to how blockchain technology can affect businesses and individuals in the near future. Banking, messaging applications, data storage, and tracking inventory are just a few.

Banking

From the big picture perspective, banks are the critical storehouse and transfer hubs of value. As a secure, digitized, and hack-proof ledger, blockchain technology can serve the same function. For blockchain technology, banking is just the beginning. This technology could provide accuracy and information-sharing to the financial service ecosystem.

Barclays and UBS, Uk-based and Swiss-based banks respectively, are experimenting with blockchain technology as a way to expedite settlements and backroom functions, which some involved in the banking industry say could cut out around $20 billion in middleman costs.

Banks are just some of the financial institutions looking into blockchain startups like R2 CEV, which works with a more than eighty member group of regulators, banks, and technology partners to create Corda, a blockchain platform being designed to be the new operating system for the financial institutions.

Messaging Apps

Telegram is a popular application amongst cryptocurrency enthusiasts because it encrypts messages to protect privacy. Currently, the founders are raising ICOs to fund the development of a blockchain platform. The decentralized messaging platform is a threat to apps such as Slack because it plans to raise the largest ICO in history, around $1.2 billion for its 170 million users. Some of the big investors rumored to be participating in this ICO are Sequoia Capital, Benchmark, and Kleiner Perkins Caufield & Byers.

Like Telegram, Kik and Line are planning to expand their cryptocurrency trading.

Hedge Funds

Numerai is a hedge fund platform backed by companies such as First Round Capital and Union Square Ventures. They're employing a plethora of traders and quants and decentralizing the operation. Numerai sends thousands of quants, separately located, and encrypts databases and asks them to build predictive models. The greatest contributors are award with a token called a Numeraire. Then, Numerai takes this strategy and makes a meta-model to create trades. In some ways, this system is a blockchain-based twist on Quantopian's model for rewarding data scientists, except there is less competition and more private collaboration.

Voting

Perhaps more understandable and close to home is voting integrity. Elections require authentication of a voter's identity, trusted tallies, and secure record keeping in order to track votes and determine the winner of an election. In the future, blockchain technology might serve as an initial structure for casting, following, and tallying votes, which could eliminate the necessity for recounts by taking voter fraud out of the picture.

By treating votes are transactions through a blockchain platform, a government and its voters can have a confirmable review trail, which ensures no votes are changed or deleted, and illegitimate votes cannot be cast. One such platform, Follow My Vote, released the alpha version of its stake-weighted and end-tend blockchain voting platform.

DNS and Internet Identity

With the current web's setup, it's difficult to determine an individual's true identity, and personal information lives on company servers for apps users use with little interoperability. uPort and Blockstack believe there is a future where an individual's identity could be easily carried with them on the internet. For example, Blockstack allows a user to access apps on top of a decentralized network and retain portability of their information.

Critical Infrastructure Security

Internet structure today has proven to be easy to hack, especially when it comes to IoT devices. As critical infrastructure security, such as transportation and power plans, all become equipped with connected sensors, the risks to our society as we know it are pretty high. Companies, such as Xage, are using blockchain's tamperproof registers to sharing security information across device networks of industrial companies.

While blockchain's ledger is public, the data transportations are sent and confirmed with advanced cryptographic techniques, which ensures information is coming from the right sources and that nothing is intercepting that information. Therefore, if blockchain is adopted more widely, the probability of hacking could lessen because the protective measures are more robust than current systems.

Some other potential uses include blockchains being used to provide large-scale data verification. For example, using the blockchain-enabled Keyless Signature Infrastructure, Guardtime - a cybersecurity startup - tags and verifies data transactions.

Ride Sharing

Applications such as Uber and Lyft represent the opposite of decentralization because both companies operate as a dispatching hub and use algorithms to control the drivers and dictate what a driver charges. Blockchain would be able to inject new options into that operation. By using a distributed ledger, drivers and riders could make a more user-driven, value-driven marketplace.

Arcade City, a startup using blockchain, supports transactions through their blockchain system. This company operates in the same way as other ride-sharing companies, but it allows their drivers to choose the rate they charge with the blockchain logging the interactions, and Arcade City takes a percentage of the fares.

This lets Arcade City appeal to professional drivers who want to build their transportation business rather than be controlled by a corporate headquarters. Drivers on Arcade City can set their rates, build their recurring customer base, and offer other services, such as roadside assistance or deliveries.

Internet Advertising

The internet you know today came about with ad hoc solutions to advertising. Ads add a lot of mobile data processing to loading a web page, and both consumers and advertisers suffer from a lack of protocols. The company Brave just ICOed their Basic Attention Token (BAT) to reimburse advertisers and viewers. Rather than having a middleman like Facebook or Google's ad arm, advertisers list directly onto the blockchain-based browser of Brave. Users are able to choose to receive fewer, but better targeted, ads without malware in them. Advertisers get better data on their budget.

Crypto Exchanges

One way a blockchain lowers the conventional cybersecurity risk is by removing the need for a human middleman. This lessens the threat of corruption, hacking, and human error. Some of the blockchain's most successful companies are centralized middlemen, and many new projects are using their own product to buy and sell blockchain-based currency by putting the entire exchange on a blockchain.

One high profile project is Enigma, which has Flybridge Capital and MIT as supporters. Enigma created Catalyst, an off-chain decentralized exchange and investment program that works without a third party as a clearinghouse. Another high-profile decentralized exchange is 0x, an Ethereum-based exchange.

Education

Academic credentials have to be universally recognized and verifiable by nature. In primary and secondary schooling and university environments, verifying academic credentials is a manual process still. It relies heavily on case-by-case verification and paper documentation.

Using a blockchain solution in education can streamline the verification process, which would reduce fraudulent claims of unearned credentials.

Sony Global Education has created an educational platform, in partnership with IBM, which uses blockchain technology to share and secure student records. Learning Machine, a ten-year-old software startup, collaborated with MIT's Media Lab to launch the Blockcerts tools that provide an open infrastructure for credentials on the blockchain.

Car Sales and Leasing

The experience of purchasing, selling, and leasing cars is a fragmented process for stakeholders on all sides of a transaction, but the blockchain technology might change this. Visa, in 2015, partnered DocuSign, a transaction management startup. This partnership sought to facilitate a proof-of-concept project that utilized blockchain technology to streamline the car leasing process, transforming the process into a click, sign, and drive procedure.

With the DocuSign tool, prospective customers were able to choose the vehicle they wanted to lease, and the transaction was entered into the blockchain's public ledger. Then, from the driver's seat, the customer would sign a lease agreement with an insurance policy, and the blockchain would update with that information. If the technology is implemented in practice, then it's not too far off to think that a process like this could be used for the sales of vehicle and registration too.

Industrial IoT and Mesh Networking

Samsung and IBM have worked on a concept called ADEPT together. ADEPT uses blockchain technology to create the backbone of a decentralized network of IoT devices. Using ADEPT, a blockchain can serve as a public ledger for a large amount of devices. In turn, these devices would no longer need a centralized hub to mediate communication between them.

Without this centralized control system to identify each other, the devices could communicate with each other autonomously to manage bugs, software updates, and energy management.

Some startups want to build blockchain technology into an IoT platform, too. As an example, Filament provides a decentralized network of IoT sensor to talk to one another. By encrypting all the way down to the hardware level and leveraging the blockchain technology, Filament's decentralized network stack lets any device to connect, interact, and transact independently of a central authority.

Cloud Storage

Often, companies offering cloud storage secure a client's data in a centralized server, which might mean increased network vulnerability from attacks by hackers. Blockchain technology cloud storage solutions let information to be decentralized, which means it is less vulnerable to hacking that can cause systemic damage and widespread loss of information.

Filecoin, which has been called the Airbnb for file storage, is a high-profile project that rewards the hosting of information. This may help make a decentralized version of S3 from the Amazon Web Services. Protocol Labs, the company behind this project, has obtained investment from Naval Ravikant, Union Square Ventures, and The Winklevosses, as well as many other prominent names. However, Filecoin is just one of numerous projects in this arena, and other token names in storage include Siacoin and Storj.

Currently, Storj is beta-testing blockchain cloud storage networks to improve their security and lessen the transaction costs of storing information in the cloud. Storj users are able to rent out any unused digital space in a peer-to-peer manner, which could create a new market for crowdsourced cloud storage capacity.

Cloud Computing

Projects based on blockchain technology, such as Golem, are letting users rent out their CPU capacity in return for tokens. Ethereum has been called the world's supercomputer due to its capability to execute smart contracts, and its mining is ASIC resistant, meaning it lets everyday computer owners compete proportionally with the big mining operations.

Forecasting

As more industries start to embrace blockchain technology, the research, consulting, analysis, and forecasting industries can be positively affected by it. If these industries have an accurate transaction recording system in place to support their data analysis, forecasting operations could have a stronger foundation for using machine learning algorithms to create targeted forecasts and insights.

Even now, blockchain is making a new predictions market. Augur, the program that uses Ethereum's blockchain technology, lets users forecast events and be rewarded for predicting those events right. The service is in beta, but the company says the process is going to be decentralized and will allow users to put bets not only on stocks and sports but on other subjects such as natural disasters and elections.

IP, Music, and Entertainment Rights

Entrepreneurs in the entertainment industry are starting to turn to blockchain technology to make content sharing easier for creators using smart contracts. The revenue on purchases of creative work is automatically distributed according to the pre-determined licensing agreements.

Mycelia was created with a focus on making intelligent songs supported by cryptocurrencies and blockchain technology. Ascribe.io, one of BigchainDB's products, works to supply a verifiable, trackable record of ownership between artists and their work.

JAAK, a British blockchain startup, has plans in the works to cooperate with music rights holders and other entertainment industry stakeholders. JAAK, which supplies an operating system for content, is creating a platform that allows media owners to convert a storehouse of metadata, media, and rights into smart content that will be able to self-execute licensing transactions on Ethereum's blockchain.

Stock Trading

Companies have been working to make the process of purchasing, selling, and trade stocks easier for years, and now blockchain-oriented startups are hoping to automate and secure the process more efficiently than any previous solution.

TØ.com, a sub-company of Overstock.com, hopes to allow stock trades online via blockchain technology. The t-zero platform merges cryptographically protected dispersed records with existing trading techniques to reduce the settlement time and the costs, as well as increase auditability and transparency.

Partnerships with trading networks and exchanges already in operation will help blockchain technology take off in the industry. Chain, a blockchain startup, is a leader on that front. Chain helped create a live blockchain integration that connected Nasdaq's stock exchange and Citi's banking organization successfully.

Real Estate

Purchasing and selling property has some snag areas, such as a lack of transparency during and after a transaction, large amounts of paperwork, errors in public records, and the potential for fraud. Blockchain can offer a way to reduce the need for record keeping on paper and speed up the transactions, which will help stakeholders advance proficiency and decrease the transaction costs on both sides of the transaction.

Blockchain technology applications for real estate can help record, track, and transfer a title, property deed, lien, and so much more, and it can help guarantee that all documents are verifiable and accurate.

Ubiquity, another blockchain startup, offers a SaaS blockchain platform for the title, financial, and mortgage companies. The company is working with Land Records Bureau in Brazil, amongst other clients, to input property information and record documents using a blockchain.

Insurance

Companies such as Tujia, Airbnb, Wimdu, and others are providing a way for individuals to temporarily exchange assets, even private homes, for a monetary value. However, the problem with this is the absence of a public record of made it almost impossible to insure assets on these platforms.

With the blockchain startup Stratumn, which allows developers to build a trustworthy application enabled by blockchain technology, professional services from Deloitte and payment services provider Lemonway were able to make public a blockchain-enabled answer called LenderBot.

A micro-insurance proof of concept for the sharing economy, LenderBot demonstrates the prospective for blockchain applications and service in the industry. LenderBot lets users enroll in customized micro-insurance through chatting on Facebook Messenger, which lets blockchain serve as the third party in the contract between users as they exchange items in the sharing economy.

Healthcare

Healthcare institutions do not have the capability to share information across platforms securely. Improved collaboration between providers might mean a higher probability of better diagnoses, effective treatments, and an overall increase in the capability of the healthcare system to deliver low-cost but effective healthcare.

The use of blockchain technology can let payers, hospitals, and other parties in the healthcare industry share access to their networks without compromising the security and integrity of the information.

Gem introduced the Gem Health Network, a blockchain network for global companies in the healthcare industry. Gem uses Ethereum's blockchain technology to make secure, universal information sharing infrastructure. Tierion is another startup using blockchain that created a platform for information storage and confirmation in the healthcare industry. Both of these companies partnered with Phillips Healthcare in the Philips Blockchain Lab.

Supply Chain Management

One of the more universally applicable components of blockchain technology is it allows more transparent, secure, and monitored transactions to take place. Supply chains are a series of transaction nodes that link together to move a product from one point to the next essentially. With blockchain technology, as products go from one point to the next across a supply chain from the manufacturer to the sale, the transactions can be logged in a permanent decentralized record. This will reduce time delays, cost, and the potential for human error.

There are many blockchain startups that are innovating in this part of the industry. For example, Provenance is creating a traceability system for products and materials, which allows businesses to participate with consumers at the point of sale with information gathered from suppliers along the supply chain.

Energy Management

Energy management's another industry that's historically been centralized. In the United States and the United Kingdom, to use energy, an individual has to go through a conventional power company such as National Grid or Duke Energy, or deal with a reseller who purchases from a big electric company.

Just like with many other industries, the circulated ledger can minimize the need for a middleman. Startups such as Transactive Grid, a joint business venture between

Consensys (a Brooklyn-based Ethereum company) and LO3 Energy, are recreating the traditional energy-exchange procedure.

Transactive Grid utilizes the Ethereum blockchain technology to allow clients to participate in decentralized energy creation systems. This allows individuals to create, purchase, and sell energy to their neighbors. LO3 Energy has operations that include Project Exergy and Brooklyn Microgrid, the former of the two being a proof of concept for gathering excess heat expelled by desktops.

Conclusion

Perhaps the mystery behind the person who originally utilized blockchain technology to make a digital currency is what has brought this revolutionary technology to light, or perhaps the world was just ready for blockchain technology to take the spotlight. No matter what it was, or if it was a combination of both, blockchain technology is here to stay. As we've explored in this book, this technology has numerous potential applications that could benefit society as a whole and investing in it now, as well as understanding it before it consumes currency and information databases as we know it, gives you an edge over the competition.

Whether you're an individual hoping to join the cryptocurrency world, or you're a business owner who wants to be a creator in that world, hopefully, the information in this book was helpful to you. If so, please help share this knowledge with other readers by leaving a review on the platform you ordered this book from.

Thank you for reading!

www.ingramcontent.com/pod-product-compliance
Lightning Source LLC
Chambersburg PA
CBHW030049230526
45471CB00003B/1002